Solitude
is a Muffled Ear

.

Poetry & Prose

Written by

Carrie Ann Wall

DEDICATION

To the Hawthorn and the RedWolf, for your straightforward honesty, unconditional friendship, generosity, and for the ever important, weed pulling garden conversations - literally, figuratively, and otherworldly - that brought me here.

To the Shadows, without you the lessons would have been missed, destined to be repeated. I am glad we can be friends.

CONTENTS

IF ONLY

If only I could paint with words
Each word selected, carefully
To construct the perfect expression of thought
My canvas this simple blank piece of paper
My pallet filled with twenty-six simple letters
placed flawlessly side by side to bring form
to the images, the emotions that well up
from the pit of my belly, like waves they flow over me
filling my chest, this need to express, to expound,
convey with precision, perfection

If only I could paint with words
There are no limits to this language
I need to break the boundaries I created,
Take it one step further, release the fire in my head
let the muses take me there, without fear
If only I could paint with words
I would paint the feelings that reside within me
with brilliant colors, and lines that caress the curves
of the mind and fill the heart and punch the gut
and take the breath away in a sudden moment
of happy delight, or wild despair, or calm peacefulness

If only I could paint with words
Then I could expel all that is within outwardly…
I would see, the depths of me,
the layers stripped away
then I… would be free

THIS CHILD

I was this child, once. The world around me was new and exciting. I wanted to touch, feel, and explore everything. I was – in the moment.

Some people, some people stop to smell the roses. A child, a child stops, and becomes the rose!

I was the rose! I was the color blue that painted the sky. I was the clouds, the sparrow, the sun, and the grass – yes, the grass. My little hands outstretched grasping the sweet smell and cooling spears. The wonder and delight of summer salts, pieces of dandelion caught in my hair, rolling down hillsides, laughing.

I was the grass and the hill and the dandelion seed that journeyed with the wind. The wind carrying me over my wonderland of curious shades of green; dark and warm, bright, and cool. And the orange fiery ball that sat high in the blue, hurting my eyes, still I look and close my eyes to see the spots.

And the beautiful gray that brought the rain. The drops of water catching in my eyelashes, trickling down my nose and finding my tongue – I was this child! My world filled with colors bright, like the birthday balloons tied to the bedpost, remnants of this child's day.

Finding sleep without struggle – awaken to the patter of my little feet, ready and waiting for what would happen next – ready and waiting…

I was this child! My world belonged to me. Every second was mine. Time, time did not exist. Nothing was contained within an hour or a minute – every moment was mine.

But only for a short time, for everything I knew to be love, every sense of security, every timeless moment, would be lost. That is when I heard it – can you hear it? That is when I heard the second hand. Time now measured - with every quick heartbeat, with every thrust of pain.

And so it began, and there I stood as the man or the boy of the foster family violated my body – my innocence suffocating, crushed under the weight of his grip. My world filled with colors bright, now blur and run together, like the chalk drawings pelted by the rain.

The gray – no longer beautiful, the drops of water, no longer playful, and the birthday balloons now deflated at the end of the bed, where this child learns to fondle the man. And there, I – this child – stood with her path of dysfunction laid out before me.

And so, I – this child – closed her eyes as the violation of her body, her innocence took place. And I, - this child – floated above the vile that sprawled out before me… and I – this child – found the rolling hills of sweet grass, my arms outstretched up to the blue…

There I spun and twirled away, faster, and faster, until this child caught the wind, that lifted this child… and I was the dandelion seed, and my world was split – between the vile and the wind.

RETRIEVAL

The souls journey recounts
of darken trails
dark as the moonless night
Blind in the pitch, eyes wide open
Seeing only shadows, watery stinging
Slowly the shadows take form
Not so scary – not good or bad
It just is - was
Returning to the place that is unsafe
cannot change the place
will not change the circumstance
cannot change the players or the play
You have been trapped here
suspended in this moment
a trauma loop, unattended
Here you will no longer stay
And so I drum a dance
and so you dance with me
I am you, you are me
Together we dance free
No longer you
You, now me

EMBRACING THE NIGHT

Dusk moves into darkness,
I sing my dreams into the sky,
like a ghostly cricket,
ringing out softly in the night

Distant birdsongs and the laughter of wolves
come swiftly to my welcoming ears
Apparently, in the deep night hours - all is well
I take up my pen and salvage things
from old pleasure ships
I cultivate some lost emotion
With the posture of youth,
personal experiences reappear

After years of change and suffering,
I see your madness in a dream
Later, perhaps, in a moment of revelation,
I will catch my own insanity, but tonight,
I will pass over my demons
allowing the sounds in the darkness
reach around and tap me gently on the shoulder

As a child, when night fell upon me,
these sounds shot fear into my hungered belly,
leaving me cold and stiff
my lost eyes, wild, searching for the dawn,
or a single ray of light

Shadows flew around me,
slowly passing over my love starved body
rendering me helpless and unable to move

Tonight, I will embrace the darkness,
leaving these nightmares behind me
I will fight pass these fears,
and look towards my dreams,
and when all is familiar and I have explored
every inch of blackness,
I will take my younger self by the hand
and lead her safely
into the night

TODAY'S TRIBE

Single mothers, stand together,
struggling, fighting to stand on two feet
Raising a child or three or four
I have seen them raise four
Alone with the cooking the cleaning,
the washing of dirty socks,
the sopping up of wet floors
Raising four and going for that Masters degree
Working two jobs and standing in the Welfare line,
standing in the Welfare line fingers pointing
screaming out "white trash"
Raising one or three or four...
alone

Alone, facing up to past dysfunctions
Heads held high proclaiming; it stops with me!
Ending the shame, ending the blame
Raising young girls to be strong women
(now there's a concept)
Raising young boys to accept and respect
without reprieve that they are more
than a walking penis
Jesus was man
Jesus was man and washed the feet of a prostitute

Today's tribe,
we are beaten and bruised, battered,
left with no sense of self, no confidence
and you...

You shower us with Prozac, send us off
to therapy and confine us with your labels

Depressive anxiety obsessive panic by-polar manic
disorder with suicidal homicidal tendencies
And her husband…
Well…he just beats her

Today's tribe,
seeking spinning, 'round and 'round
standing up, stepping forward and losing ground
Slipping, slipping, slipping through the cracks
dissolving revolving through,
melting into a pot of numbers
Statistics have shown…
statistics have shown that you have lost us
in the shuffling of papers,
and we become,
the movie of the week

Today's tribe, my tribe
Found me broken, without choice, without voice
lost with in a twisted up, tangled up mess
and the baggage was heavy
Pulling me down, swinging me 'round
to the edge of sanity
Oh, to die!
To die would be peace

But you caught me
You took me in your arms and you held me

I kicked, I screamed, I pushed and pushed,
and you held me
I cried, I fumbled, I fucked up,
and you held me
and here I stand,
alive!

My tribe,
with you I have come out of the pit of despair,
out of being helpless
and into being hopeful
and here I stand
a single mother, facing up, head held high,
proclaiming – it stops with me!

THE DYING BREED

We are a dying breed,
the free thinker
I am going to place this
in your hands
My life, my dreams
are beyond the norm of labels
beyond that television set
We sit, we stare
as it sucks us dry
There are not many free thinkers left
We are a dying breed
Let it stop here!
It stops with me, it stops with you
Have you stopped to look at the sky?
I did
It is limitless
I soared into its blues, its pinks
Its orange glow of a fallen sun
We are explorers
Explode into your fears, your dreams
Explode out of this societal bondage
Cross that line into the free thinker
We are a dying breed
You are the life force
which could allow us to live forever
in body, in spirit, in thought

I have lived the life of fools
I have lived with that talking box
that stands as the center of the family unit
that glowing, pulsating nucleus
that spoon feeds its victims cancer
I have swallowed its regurgitated Cindy Crawfords
It leaves a bitter taste in my mouth
Can you taste it?
Can you smell the rotting vomit?
It is sitting there on our coffee tables
and in our children's laps

I took a flight
over our welled groomed neighborhoods
I saw the man carefully tending to his lawn
in the morning light
seeing to the weed that placed itself
in the center of his seeded grass
He is missing the dawn
I am the dawn and all its spectacular colors
I am that transformation into another day
and the man…
carefully tends to his lawn

I have lived the life of mothers
who rush to make the meals on time
who rush to sanitize the children
who rush…
to dust that vomit on the coffee table

I took a lesson from my smallest student
being no more than three
Standing there in my germ-free kitchen
making my germ-free meal
This beautiful spirit looking up at me
This creature I have very little understanding of
becomes the teacher
and is no longer the student

Out of the steam rising from the boiling pots
and the sound of the timer going off
and among the burnt dinner rolls
my teacher says
"Mama, there are stars in your pocket"
"See the stars, Mama?"
Pulling an invisible star from my pocket
the teacher holds it up to show me
"See the star Mama?"
I saw that star that day
I saw much more than that
I saw past the chaos,
beyond the sanitation
of this America
I saw through these false freedoms
Through the eyes of my child
my teacher,
I saw,
the dying breed

TRAIN RIDE HOME

Drunken lovers seated in the front
I glance and watch, my loneliness swells
Rising, falling, rising again

My attentions turn to the swearing and cursing
coming from the back
"I got myself a fucking faggot!", I hear him say
They frighten me as they walk past
beer cans and swollen egos swagger by
I do not make eye contact or glance

A rush of cool air takes me back to the city
Collages of sounds, car horns and bustling people
Moments of hesitating panic, "Where did they go?"
I see Stephen, tall in stature and panic leaves,
my eyes lock on his image

His umbrella hangs from his arm
He is always in character, always precise
saunters, floats at times
I see him and think… London or France
He is in novels and poems
written by Whitman or Radcliff Hall
I could lose him easily
but never forget,
we all move on

"Babylon!" the conductor shouts down the aisles
The squealing clanking of metal and steal, jerks me back

Lovers giggle and kiss, drunks speak
in chopped up sentences, words slur with a twist

Warm smells with a chill
Diesel, I think - or hot metal
I want to close my eyes and dream
Song after song rattles off in my head
Broadway settles into my heart
and I am satisfied, mesmerized
I want to go back, I want to sleep
Once again, we are in motion

My traveling companion bobs his head
We cannot sleep for fear of missing our stop
I want to put my head on his shoulder,
settle into his warmth
I doze, he nudges me back
Moments later, I return the nudge

I think of Greg standing outside the theater
His intense silence before the show
His eyes don't focus on any one thing
He is above the rush of people,
beyond the neon flashes
His distance leaves me uncertain
but it is brief,
his expression and delight returns,
once the stage is set
I could lose him easily, but never forget
We all … move on

STEPHEN

I lost a treasure today
I went frantically looking for it
To another, it would not seem so…important
Just a tattered and stained fast food menu,
the receipt still stapled at the top
I cannot find it – how can it be lost
I remember it well
every detail
Sitting at Greg's kitchen table
scratching out a poem
of our journey to Broadway – the songs, the lights
still bright in our eyes

"five hundred twenty-five thousand six hundred minutes…"

The poem, is no longer fresh in my mind
but you are
How I wish I could find that tattered menu
The memory of you, still attached to it
Stephen, my dearest friend… you left a mark in my life
You made a difference
I only wish… I had been there
to make a difference in yours
I lost a treasure today
Frantically I went looking for it
But you… you were gone
We all… move on

WHITMAN'S EXAMPLE

Never have I loved a man more
then that of he,
whose leaves gently fell,
into hands from dusty shelves
Whose words whispered
sweet of life, intoning hymns
of self-affection
He who bravely witnessed death
He who "held the space"
for sons and daughters
of His America
Understanding "holding space"
long before the phrase devised

BAR SIDE

Loneliness seeps out of the skin
and lingers in the smoke-filled air
Swirling 'round the disco lights
and clinging to the walls

Smile lines, crease out hidden sadness
Isolation and damnation
has brought us here
Lost loves and broken hearts gather
to sing, to dance, to drink
to forget, or to remember

In a world of boy meets girl
we sit bar side
Boy, boy
Girl, girl
In hopes of a glance or a dance
I travel an hour on the off chance
that SHE may be there

The sudden burst of laughter
A brief moments of silence
as the juke box changes its song

The old man who watches from the corner
the tight young bodies of boys dancing close
Following the hand that slides down chest
placing itself on hip

The bull dyke who leans back in chair
cigarette lit, ready to defend
her sacred space
leaving no trace of her insecurities

The misfits and leaches
who scan the room
zoning in on their next target
The target
beaming out naïve innocence

We mix and mingle
Gossip travels from ear to ear
Drunks stumble through the crowd
weaving by, breaking glass
and we laugh

In a world of boy meets girl
we sit bar side
Boy, boy
Girl, girl
In hopes we find our way out

THE PERFECT MATCH

For the first time in my life, I am alone
Not alone in the sense that there is no one but
alone in that there is no partnership
I share my space with no one, but I am not alone,
for the voices in my head that were once
drowned out by the needs and wants of others
and my foolish desire to please
those voices began to shout and yell

The voices boomed into my ears, blood began to run,
dripping from the drumming and ringing in my mind
 – this self-imposed solitude – it hurt
Hurt so much that at times I felt pulled back to others
– others to drown out the racket in my head
others who I could please, with ease,
simply give up my voice and echo the influence
of words, opinions, dreams, schemes, pain – their pain,
I could ease while all a long neglecting, denying my own

It was easier to sit among the chatter of others
then to sit alone with myself – ignoring the self,
reflecting only what was opposite of me
 – if only I could be like them –
I might be deserving of love because
they are loved and confident and interesting
 – if only I could be like that, like them – not like me

I have always been one part of two
that should have equaled a whole,

but it was never equal, and I was never whole
Instead, I was a fourth or a third –
I was fractured by the fractions that
divided itself by itself and the other until I felt like a
zero
and so I ran

Leaving in my wake a list of blame and fault –
not mine but theirs
because they had neglected me and my needs
fleeing so fast, not stopping until
I ran into the arms of another
and so the circle and cycle began again
and I could reflect only what was in front of me
not project what was inside of me
and the arms that wrapped around me were always
narcissistic not once realizing
I was their perfect match

Always the victim of what was wrong with them
and I could fix them, mold them, hold them
so tight until they behaved as they should
and when it didn't work, I ran again and again
I could not understand why…

Why I could not find the right person
who would make me happy,
Leaving my happiness to their care,
how unfair – to lay the impossible upon their shoulders

You see, I grew up believing,
you are not one without the other
and if you stand alone,
then there must be something wrong
and so I fell for the first thing that took interest
and how lucky am I
that someone might like me or even love me
and they say take it slow, get to know them...
Not take it slow, get to know yourself, know yourself

So not knowing myself for years
I tried to fit myself into someone else's mold
and when I did not fit – it cracked
and so I believed there must be something wrong –
with me.

I'm not pretty enough or smart enough or
interesting enough
because I cannot hold your interest and
you don't see me
See me! See me!

But it was not their fault, they were not to blame
They played the game – I lured them in –
falsifying the self – to reflect them
but that reflection falls apart quickly
and the victim emerges –
its easier to blame than it is to be accountable

And so, when I found myself once again,
feeling dissatisfied, victimized, unhappy and criticized

I began to fantasize
What would it be like to be alone
To only be responsible for me

And over a period of years
I fancied the idea more and more
It was an idealistic notion
and I envisioned a strong, independent woman
that needed no one
Who could do it – this life – alone
 Leaving the longest relationship, I ever had,
years of a comfort zone that brought little comfort –
how grand this would be – I would be free…to be me
So, sitting alone for the first time in my new place – I
cried

For three days the tears streamed down my face
and I thought this is a mistake –
it's a mistake! I should go back –
this silence is so loud
and the thoughts in my head
were like static flashing in between the fuzz –
the voices screaming all at once
"See me, see me, see me!"

And I saw myself –
it was not that strong, independent woman
I had envisioned –
but just a child, unsure and scared

It was hard – getting to know myself
Accepting fault, acknowledging mistakes –
harder still – forgiveness of self, seeing my strengths,
loving who I am with all my imperfections

Slowly, as I began to listen to the inner voices,
the silence was not so loud,
the scared, unsure child became curious,
pushing through the voices that did not belong
A peacefulness arose and flowed through me
and into everyday life

But don't be fooled
I was never truly alone
Between the time of the thoughts of leaving
and actually leaving –
this journey to the self, had already begun
You see when you begin to figure out who you are –
they appear, unjudgmental and accepting
Perfectly matched friendships are forged,
bringing strength, lessons, and unconditional love
And so, some two years later,
I am standing in the mirror, lovingly…
projecting the reflection, in front of me

STANDING STILL

Frozen, still standing, stuck
The moving world – spins on
The mind – orbits, opposite
Background chanting
        The have to's…
        The to do's…
        The should of, the could of…
The mud, boots thick
Can only lean so far
Reaching…for what?
Hard thinking, is heavy work
        Just move…
        Move!
Abandon the boots
Look up – look out
Come back – reset, be present
Struggle, wiggle free the feet
Come back for the boots
Better still…
leave them to the mud

PASSING THROUGH

I have taken from those who pass through my life,
gathering up bits and pieces, making myself whole
Learning life's lessons has never been easy
but the lessons of life have always been those moments
of inspiration and revelation
A retrospect that brings me closer to my point of being

If I could hold in my hand every ounce of pain
that has been inflicted upon me
I would be holding the essence that
makes me who I am today
For from within that pain has sprouted forth
glorious energies of strength and courage,
compassion and an undying yearning
for growth and spiritual beginnings

If I could hold in my other hand every bit of joy
people passing through have given me,
I would be holding an overwhelming peacefulness
that would satisfy me for a life time

Combined these two things together
the pain and the joy,
I hold all that makes me who I am today
All that is dear and precious
All that is strength

If I can say, I have learned
then I say,
I am grateful to have met you
No matter what you bring as you pass through
I will carry it down my path
You are my teachers and I, the willing student

CIRCLE IN THE DARKNESS

Trees in the shadows stand tall against the night sky
their leaves dance, sway with the tender breeze
Our bodies move as they move,
they move as we move
like a child asleep on mother's chest
breathing in rhythm
We are encircled in the darkness,
damp soft moss at our feet
The fireflies dance in the distance
the fireflies kiss our noses
the fireflies pop here and there
the Moon sits low in the sky
She plays hide and seek among the trees
My spirit awakens in this sacred circle
My spirit spins and plays
My spirit takes flight, kisses the Moon
She returns my kisses with gentle beams of light
My mind's eye opens
the ground beneath my feet falls away
the sky opens into infinite space
I am home, I am at peace
I am here, I am there
I am above, I am below
I am the moon beam, I am the Moon
I am the gentle breeze
I am the trees, I am the dancing leaves
I am…
I am…
I am…

CONTROLLED MOVEMENT

Momentum builds
Each foot forward
leads me to the edge,
falling back on heals, with a sudden stop
Standing at the precipice, like The Fool
without a single foolish thought in my head
It has been a winding road
Its beginnings starting long before
the path was ever found
Like the serpent that sheds its skin
Many skins lay far behind me now
I contently leave them
Momentum builds
each foot forward
leads me to the edge
No need for a gentle push
for I will gladly leap

A YEAR AND A DAY

I placed my foot upon this path,
and trembled a bit
The excitement overflowing,
for I have searched for this road for many years
And now,
I stand here with you
at a turning point
We cannot see what is around the bend
and the steps we have already taken
cannot be turned about

We have traveled a bit,
you and I
And now,
here we stand…
changed, changing, shifting
breaking molds, taking flight,
finding sight, sound,
hearing our hearts call to this path
and we have traveled
one year and a day
and here we stand…
changed, changing
creating shifts of our own making
creating change
creating changes
creating

Nothing will ever be the same again
You and I…
will never be the same again
Our hearts grow stronger,
our thoughts break through
all that old glue that kept us stuck and sticky
tact down and bound – our freedom now found

The Moon shines brighter
The Sun climbs higher
The Trees speak louder
The birds, snakes, stags and bears
all creatures big and small now speak to us
in dreams and waking life and
we have traveled a bit
you and I
Just a year and a day and
we have learned to pray, to chant
to lend our hearts to the healing art of self
Taking those old wounds down from the shelve
learning to heal and feel in different ways
those wounds close up, one by one
their lessons done

And now,
to move on to the next
for the learning never ends
the road continues to bend

But we have been guided…
We depart from here, free of fear
for the Silver Tipped Raven stands at the center
showing us the way…and we have learned from
the Wolf to navigate with swifts steps
and we are guarded by the Hawthorn, who protects
her delicate flowers, that will change into solid beings
and we have learned from the NightHawk
who guides us in flight with keen sight
and we have learned from the StarOwl
whose wisdom is endless and deep
and we are guided by the Dragon whose Amber Heart
glows bright in dark places
and we have learned from the RedWolf who
teaches us to tread, through the Forest Black
and we have learned from the WebWeaver
how to walk with the Shadows
and we have learned from the Serpent
how to set the Fire in the black Onyx night
and we have learned from the ShadowWolf
how to hunt down our passions found
and we have learned from Lord Krogan,
who has taught us to face our fears, without the tears,
and stand strong and true
and we have learned from the Willow
who stands strong against the rain,
her branches never breaking,
but only bend with the winds of change
and we have learned from the Ivy
that climbs to high places, always finding a way
and we have learned from the Autumn Moon,

whose full bellied light shows our uniqueness
and we have learned from the River
that flows freely with the contours of the land
and together we stand, hand in hand
bound by the call to this path
and I…
I am honored to stand here with you

Yes, we have traveled a bit, you and I
Just a year and a day
and here we stand
forever changing,
forever changed

THE DESCENT

In the shade of shadows, I sit and wait
for the hush whispers from each direction
They appear to question and test my faith
in their eyes I see my own reflection
"No! Not good enough" these harsh words I hear
Come down the walls I worked so hard to build
They crumble away revealing my fears
The power of legends are now revealed

My mind's eye spins like whirling dancers
I fight to be humble and not so proud
I do not struggle to find the answers
but for the courage to speak them aloud
From North to East to South to West I stand
to receive the gifts from each sacred shrine
A Stone, a Spear, a Sword, a Cup in hand
I return each treasure to the Divine

Slowly I descend to the depths of Hel
where my Lady tends to death and dying
Ushering them through with a Banshees wail
The tears wash over me with a cleansing crying
Despairing is the loss of love and life
But only death can bring rebirth
and my Lord freely gives his sacrifice
for his death gives life as he returns to the earth

I am transformed as She was transformed
There is nothing more certain than change
I am reborn as He was reborn
and nothing remains the same

A STRANGE SILENCE

What expression can be found
Lost within a thought
Not a thought but a sensation
Not a sensation
but a drop of emotion
Not a drop but a rain
filling vast oceans
Mysterious, complexing
Solitude is a muffled ear
Inward focus – a ringing
low and faint
The head slightly tilting
Straining to hear, to understand
Eerie is the breathing
of my own breath
Rhythmic thumping
of blood through veins
Again, the ear strains
Frozen in a moment
of strange silence
Nothing moves
but the pen

MENDING BRANCHES

On top a hillside, set against the horizon, sat a magnificent oak tree. Her beauty bounded from her roots to her limbs. Her branches stretched out strong towards the sky and in the spring her beautiful leaves danced in the wind. With every passing season her roots grew deeper, feeding on the rich soil of the earth. She was a strong tree. Standing tall and proud. Those who gazed upon her, delighted in her glory, seeing wisdom in every new sprouting leaf. Each bud added to her story. Each limb, unique.

The oak had seen many seasons and she stood unmoved against the gusting winds of winter, and un-withered against the scorching sun of August. In the fall, her saplings would journey with the wind finding moist soil to begin new growth, creating lush forests. She was the mother of many, a symbol of death and rebirth. Each dying leaf that fell in the fall gave way to the sprouts of new branches in the spring. Never had there been a more perfect tree.

One night, in late spring, a cold and blustery wind blew across the land, bringing with it heavy rain. The oak tree had seen many storms but never one quite like this. The relentless rain angrily pounded her newly sprouted branches. Slowly the temperature began to drop, and the rain turned to sleet. Her branches began to freeze, and the weight of the icy frozen water brought her outstretched limbs bowing to the ground. Her highest point nearly touching the earth below. She fought hard against the storm. Her roots gripped the soil, like a hand squeezing tight, holding her trunk upright. With all her might she stood unmoved through the storm until finally the wind began to slow. The clouds parted into a chilly night sky. Her icy branches glistening in the moonlight.

As the sun rose, you could hear her strain against the weight of the ice. In the distant forests came the eerie popping noise of branches bending and breaking. As a gentle breeze swept through the air, an orchestra of wind chimes would sound out as the icy limbs clattered against each other. The storm left in its wake many trees damaged and dying. Many trees could not hold tight and uprooted. Some could not hold the weight of the ice and split down their center, destroying their very core. The big oak was not left unharmed. Although she fought bravely to keep all her branches intact, there was one young limb that fell victim to the ice. The limb split away and fell helplessly below her, landing at the base of the big oak's trunk. The oak wept quietly for many moons, grieving her loss.

The loss of her limb was painful, but the oak continued to grow and change with the seasons. As you know, she was a strong tree. Slowly the damage from the fallen limb healed but still the scar remained. She was still a beautiful tree, but there was a noticeable gap in her queenly crown. Little did she know, the falling limb that lay below her, began to take root.

After the storm, the young limb began to thaw with the warmth of the sun. The little limb felt the loss of the support system of the big oak and longed to find her way back. As the limb took root, she grew stronger with every passing season. She stretched up for the sky with all her might and rooted deep into the soil. Many winter winds blew across the land and many summer suns bared down on the little limb. But the limb stood unmoved and un-withered, just as the big oak. Soon, the limb was no longer a limb. She was a tree of her own. Sprouting new branches in the spring and letting go of her leaves in the fall.

One late spring morning, the big oak stretched out her high branches and opened her newly sprouted leaves. She felt a sudden change in her leafy crown. The gap that had been there for many years was full of young branches. She saw that the young limb she had lost years ago, grew to be a tree right beside her. This young tree grew to be strong and beautiful just like her.

Two became one, even more magnificent than before. Their leaves dancing together in the morning breeze. Their crown was so big you could see it from miles away. Together, they became the most perfect tree in all the land. Those who gazed upon them marveled at their beauty. The big oak, whole once again.

PHOTOGRAPH

The flesh that wraps about my frame
rib of your rib
grew from seed, from egg of you
and you from theirs
and theirs from them
from them – from distance cells
long grown – youth to dust
Faces set behind the glass
frozen in just that moment
thoughts lingering on the flash
Best dressed in pearls, hair soft and neat
lips gently curled, slight the smile
with hopes of remembrance
And so, you sit, from seed, from egg
of them and theirs to me
Behind the glass, I see…
the flesh that wraps about my frame

DAVID'S PEAR

To hear a voice that has not echoed in my mind
in ages… is a strange thing
I start to fall backwards into memories
with the smooth rich tone of your words
I was… rough around the edges then
You were…beautiful and infuriating
I was sure you were destined for great things
and I was… close to falling fast
into the disparity of my own creation
To hear your voice again is… calming
and the recall of you reminds me…
it was you who opened up my world
Campbell, Ginsburg, Dali, Dylan
Those are no small things, my friend
and your sincere kind words the last we spoke
was enough to leave regret behind me

MOVING FREELY

The movement of freedom
to move freely wherever my feet will carry me
plotting to trot, to run, to skip, to play
to move freely
I am constricted in this social disorder,
made to tread with the machine
some invisible apparatus holds me in my place
I am just one bolt in this giant turning engine
slowly rusting, crusting over becoming corroded
I must move freely, break free from this structure
before I have no more threads to twist away

Oh, the movement of freedom
I felt it once in its purity
I remember it well …
I felt like I could fly, could soar to any height
the feeling of moving freely
walking down Main Street
I cut the strings and set out to make my own mistakes,
freely

Sleeping in the park,
making love on roof tops,
a freedom choice
weekend trip to New York city with only thirty bucks
hairy armpits, weed and cloves,
patchouli scented hair and bells on my ankles
a freedom choice
dancing, drumming, strumming down Elmwood

Wednesday nights at Broadway Joes
Saturdays at Hallwalls
Salvador Dali hanging on the wall
Jerry filling my head with his Bird Song
Strawberries with Shakespeare in the park
Wild Irish Rose on a warm stormy night
It was a fleeting flight
But oh, how I was free
no matter how naïve it may have seemed
I was…
moving freely

I long to move freely again
but with wisdom beneath my feet
I long to break away from this machine
that keeps me in my place
conformity has become an enemy
it will not let loose of me
How I long for the movement of freedom
to move freely, wherever my feet will carry me

LEFT FOOT, RIGHT SHOE

I cannot let you in
You, who lives in my neighborhood
who gives me my change
or checks my ticket
or holds the door open for me
You who smiled, politely inquiring
I cannot let you in
I am awkward in this skin

A left foot in a right shoe
A backwards sweater
that looks right but feels odd
A simple twist around
it is properly worn
I am never properly worn

Outwardly, all is well
Yet there is a frantic inside turning
The tag never finding its place
I assume you know this
Comfort comes only with the familiar
The familiar, taking years to bring comfort

For those who found their way in
You did not climb over
A crack found to squeeze in
I know you got stuck in your efforts
But still, you made it through
I am grateful you did

Now, my walls are more than just brick
Surrounded by those who were patient
Surrounded by those who waited
The cracks intentionally left
But you, the unfamiliar
who smiled kindly, politely inquiring
I cannot let you in
I am much too awkward in this skin

COSMIC JANET AND THE UNIVERSAL DEPRESSION

You were a spark so unique and so different
You wore your suffering on your sleeve
It was beautiful and terrifying
all in one breath
Your piercing blue eyes - captivating
I was held there, in your space
I knew it intimately, every crevice, every corner
even that which was hidden from the world
You shared it with me among coffee cups
and cigarette smoke, sitting around the table
for hours, laughing, crying
swimming in the pool of our universal depression
That is what Janet called it
We would linger there
it was a fine vat of slime and muck
filled with childhood terrors
Slowly, I found my way to the surface
I held tight to your hand – but you slipped away
back down into the abyss
Your pain too heavy – holding you down
I knew your suffering – it was real
Today I woke up to find, that you are now at rest
Your suffering ended
may you remain always in peace, my love,
we will, meet again

FIRESIDE

 "We were as tall as the grass, but the trees outgrew us"

Burning pine….
The sent encircles around us,
twirling thru the nostrils
Memory sensory kicks in childhood triggers
I can see you here, at this place
Your child spirit lingers still and plays and runs
and even after you are long gone,
beyond these earthly bonds,
you will still remain here
For you have spoken the stories out loud
around the fire and your memories
are etched in my mind
As we sit fireside,
we will create our own moments,
that will echo through these woods,
and be carried with the wind
This place and all the energy that flows within it
inspires me to take up my pen
For five years nothing has flowed
from my hand to the paper, until now
For five years I have not felt
like myself, until now
Tonight, sitting fireside with you, I have awoken
and become self-aware,
under this star filled skies,
among the trees and the grass
and the beautiful spirit that is you

MY NIAGARA FALLS

Unending hues of color
shuffle down, descend with facets of grey
Peaceful floating above cascading clouds
A gentle breeze, the deceiving taste
of the chilling blue oceans and green seas
The violence of the water crashing into the rocks
The silent rush before the roar

Shuffling feet,
the flash and clicks of the curious camera
Echoes of a foreign tongue, a known tongue
The fascination of the children's eyes
the dying's eyes, the artist, poet's
and working man's eyes
all whose perception,
quite different from my own

The passing of lovers
Old love replenished with the waters endless age
New love enveloped with the powerful boom
Stale love dying with the smashing of the rocks

This is my Niagara Falls
All my hopes and dreams diminish
with the rolling, falling water
Only to be reborn, with the cooling rain
and the tiniest of creek and brook

WELLS DEEP

What was once known
holds no more sway on this moment
of fingertips punching
where once ink ran from callused digits
I am wells deep in history
Steeped in a dysmorphic sense of self
The well now overflows
flooding over, trickling at first
into streams, growing into rivers
raging into rapids – moving away
from what was known, plummeting over
jagged rough edges, the power of motion
smoothing sharp rock
Falling into crystal clear pools
were reflection mirrors back this moment
What was once thought of self
holds no sway – as this is the gift of water, of wells
Wishes left behind of stone, of coin
Moving into action – forward motion
to the sea, to the ocean – cleansing, clearing
Swelling waters, washing away falsehoods
of what was thought of self
no longer drowning
no longer sinking
Peacefully floating
riding a top the waves

THE DEPTHS

I step to the edge of the shore
The sounds of the beach goers fade
I hear only the chattering of the gulls
as the waves break at my feet
I am drawn to you, pulled by the tide
Further I step over shell and rock
Further I move into you

The cool immersion sends away
the heat of the noon day Sun
I rock - sway with an easy motion
I look out at your vast existence
I am in awe
What world lies beneath your waves

Deep, deep into an abyss I will never know
None will ever know, for we have not
mastered your furthest depths
What wonders there must be
closest to our Mother's core

I close my eyes, even now as I recall
I am pulled down, deeper still
into the deepest depth of my being
The waves of past emotions
move through and around me
Deeper still they change - dissipate

She calls to me to look deeper still
Weightlessness…
there is freedom here

Weightlessness…
she washes away the heaviness of my burdens
If only I dare to go deeper still
What wonders there must be
closest to My core

I step to the edge of the shore
The vastness of possibilities
wait at my feet

THE BODY ACHES

The body aches
Not from the depth of sadness
or the darkness of depression
that stiffens the bones
tires the heart

The body aches with
wonderful movements
The stroke of the paintbrush
steps of walking
slamming of the hammer
buzz of the chainsaw
digging of dirt

Exhaustion comes
The bed hugs the tired limbs
the throbbing knees
Sleep settles in
The body repairs

Glorious is the stretch
that greets the dawn
The body aches into the passions
of another day, happily aching

Creating takes hard movements
I appreciate the ache

YOUTHFUL PROMISE

Youth came for a visit
Oh, how the Trees laughed!
Their roots stretching towards
open hearts with hopeful promise
The fire danced, light of foot
flames leapt, skipped about
with the voices of future wisdom
The Crows fell silent, ears open
allowing Youth to wash away
the heaviness of aged experience
The Earth smiled, hoping to heal
with the changing generation
Joyful at the possibility,
of a new collective dream

BIRD LOVE

Vibrant colors come to me daily
I sit rocking, thoughtfully in my chair
Hours of yellow, red, black, white,
countless shades, brown and orange
Time slips away into a space of
peaceful smiling
My spirit lifts with the fluttering of wings
My heart beats with the drumming of beaks
My head fills with the many
Cheerily, cheer-up, what-chew, wit, wit, wit
per-chick-o-ree, jay-jay, chick-a-dee-dee-dee notes
with the occasional caw-caw-caw
heard from high above
From behind the glass I watch and listen
My wheels stop spinning
Self-talk is silenced
All troubles fall away
With this
my bird love

A GIFT FOR A GIFT

Hum, buzz, flutter – tweet
What joy is this?
A flash, a shimmer
Just at the edge of my sight
Turning to look – you are gone
Just as those moments in memory
filled with exhilaration
A new love
Hot electricity rushes quickly
from toe to head
Always brief – and forgotten
Then you appear – just out of view
What a delightful little dance we dance
until, finally - you are in front of me
You hold me there – suspended on tiny wings
Nose to beak, we are lifted
together we journey
between worlds
You continue to return - time and again
to the sweet water
A gift for a gift
A divine exchange
that only you and I
need to understand

SUMMER'S END (INSPIRED BY THE FROST)

My basket is full
The harvest busting out the sides of woven reeds
I carry it into the promised chilled air of September
So many… lessons, losses, gains,
my arms buckling under the weight of summers fullness
let loose and fall into memory
Just as the weight of the apple,
allows it to break free from its branch
The seeds of new branches, lay waiting within the fruit
The branch, relieved of its burden
Oh, how I gather up!
Take inventory of ripened fruit
Weary not from the gathering,
But from the weight of all that I have gathered
Open wide my arms!
So that they may be emptied, to rest, for a time
until the next Summer's fullness, fills them up again

SHIFTING SEASONS

Somber is the cooling air and falling leaves
The green fading away into earthly tones
The sun low, just at the horizon
Orion appears in the west
clearly defined among the stars
Hazy skies turn crisp and brittle
Another season makes an appearance
and there is a shift, a change, a swing
My mind turns inwards, indoors,
to hearth and home
I treasure this shift
Without it there would be no contemplation
on what was, what is, and what will be
Hidden secrets will make themselves known
Time for study, for prose, for prayer
Somber is the cooling air and falling leaves
I am wrapped in the warmth of reflection

IT MATTERS NOT

It matters not what chair I sit
Or which four walls surround me
Nor the latitude in which I stand
My thoughts, myself, I cannot flee
The steam that rises from the cup
Matters not the herb it steeps
Same is the breath, inhales the scent
No secrets of the self can keep
As winter's silence falls around me
I muse the life that I created
The strife, the struggle, the success
All that keeps me sharp and sated
Whether I am here or there
As above, the same below
Changes come with lessons learned
Myself moves with me as I go
And so with winter all around me
I contemplate with cup in hand
What four walls will surround me
And which direction I will stand

REMEMBERING SPRING

At winters end
the spring snows begin
Yesterday's promised sun
fades quietly into memory
If not for the Robin
one might forget...
winter ends... when the spring snows begin

MEETING MS. COLETTA

I met you
even though we never met
You are remembered
the land does not forget
Your sweat, your blood
words and actions
left its mark up on the hill
You came to me
through the memories of others
From beyond the grave
you inspire
And so,
you are remembered

TIME

I sit in awe of this strange shifting life
And marvel at the thoughts of existence
What complaints have I with such little strife,
My struggles caused by my own resistance
Time passes without judgment or caring,
Moving forward without trepidation
It is unforgiving and so unsparing
And has no center or destination
O, such little time we have to wander
Among the wild birds and untamed beasts
With wasteful movements my time is squandered,
While looking for crumbs, I've missed the feast

       I vow to join the bountiful table
       No longer lingering underneath

SAVING THE WORLD ON SUNDAY MORNINGS

Sister friends
Drum drum drumming
Ideas forming
sacred smoke, clearing
binaural beats humming
In this space between worlds
we are brave
In a space created for creating
In a space transformed
Flowing from the heart to the heart
healing thought forms appear
The hurting world flows over
into the empathy that is our gift
At times our curse
In this space
on Sunday mornings
before the dawn
between sips of coffee
and swirling incense smoke
We save the world
For just one singular moment
with the flash of an atomic ping
all life stops suffering
Peace and joy
Love and gratitude
culminates in fantastic bursts
of laughter
of tears

Laying waste to the hate
the fear
that permeates
into the hearts of all
manufactured
and distributed
perfectly engineered fear…
is cleared
But as the sun rises
The smoke dissipates
The world wakes
Dreams fade into the fog
All begins again
And we, my Sister friend
will save the world
on the next, Sunday morning

SPIRIT DRIVEN

Baton strikes stretched skin
where once the heart pumped blood
to lungs, to liver, to spleen
Spirit driven through low rhythm
Foot to shoulder – moves to transform
from hoof to horn – moves to transform
from wing to beak – moves to transform
Back again, hand to shoulder
to shoulder, to shoulder...
ten-thousand times over – connected
by the rhythm of stretched skin
Connected by hands stretched out
on rocks in dark caves
Reaching out through the ages
reaching out across time, across moments
Stretching the skin, kin to us all
All connected...
Where once the heart pumped blood...
to lungs, to liver, to spleen

BALCONY SONGS – 3/17/2020

A metal pot and lid rings out
An instrument of joyful childhood beats
Banging out tunes with clapping hands
Tap, tap, tapping – from balconies
Voices raise up –
accordions squeeze out melodies and
they sing, sing, sing
No matter the song –
the air fills with hope, with healing
to those in tents, under thin silver blankets
They sing out in unity – connecting through distance
Connected by separation –
their songs, killing desperation
Barriers break on their open-air stages
becoming one voice with their song
Booming applause ripples through their city,
gratitude abounds
Swinging 'round street corners, finding its way
to those in hazmat suits and paper masks
Ten years from now, these images, these sounds
we will remember… recount how they sang…
everyday - at noon and at five
sheltered in place, united together,
bringing healing and hope
with their balcony songs

SHOOTING STAR

I saw a shooting star,
It shot across the sky
So fast, so beautiful
Like the moments we had together

It fell into my mind,
A trapped image, there to be remembered
Just as you fell into my heart

I wished upon the falling light,
For happiness, for love
I wished for you to hold me,
Forever and a day

But the light had gone so quickly,
Just as you
No chance to say I love you
No chance to say good-bye

MOON WORK

The New Moon,
sets a time to be
in silence 'til
the day of three

Waxing Moon,
the mother grows
Bring towards you and
work the flow

Full Moon,
has the greatest power
Draw her down
Watch magic flower

Waning Moon,
reverse the flow
Removes all obstacles
Let things go

THE WORD

I wander through the thoughts aroused
Are they my own
or echoes of places past
I remember not

Whispers set upon my ear
Long lost ideas repeated
What was the original word?
The first syllable
The utterance of creation

Not a "bang"
or a booming to shatter the drum
But rather a vibration
a low hum, hesitating at first
perfection practiced
not a stutter
but a patient, careful curl
of tongue and lip

In the beginning there was The Word
A single distinct expressive element
of sound – conception
The Word - to name a thing
Naming - shared understanding
That which separates animal
from hominid

The Word - so much power lies within it
creator of stars, of heavens, of histories
maker of gods, of heroes, of hell
The Word – paints landscapes, crumbles mountains
calls legions, defeats devils
proclaims love, invokes violence

The Word – creator
How careless we have become
with such power

IF YOU LIKE ME

If you like me, hit like, and copy and paste on your wall.
If you don't like me hit like and copy and paste on your wall.

If you don't like to like things, then comment below.
If you like me but don't want to copy and paste then hit like and tell me in a comment below that you don't like to copy and paste things on your wall.

I will be watching this post all day, so I know that
I am likable and can measure my own self-worth.
So don't make me feel bad and hit like.

If you hate cancer, give me an Amen
and copy and paste to your wall.

If you want Donald Trump as our next president...
keep scrolling.

If you want lots of money to come you than hit love
and then start working harder.

If you are unhappy hit "WOW" and happiness will
come but seriously.... hit like if you like me and
comment below how wonderful and awesome I am,
then give me a "Ha-ha" and ...

Realize that Facebook is not a place where you will find your true friends... they are but a phone call away, pick up the phone and use your voice and words to talk to someone today.

It will change your life –
Hit like if you agree and give me a "LOL" and an Amen.

KAREN

Dear Karen, I am sorry
Sorry that your good name was taken
taken and applied to behaviors that need no name
other than simply bad
A bad public display of a reaction, to a situation
with underlining causes
that no one will ever stop to find
or even try to understand

Always, only giving a one-sided camera view
of what might be, one of the worse moments
of a person's life, when crushing pressure
the weight of one's own struggles collapses
upon and explodes outwardly toward those
holding up their phones, pressing re-cord

Never capturing the trigger that took place
only a moment before, or hours earlier, or years prior
Sending that one momentary collapse into a void
only to be retrieved, viewed and multiplied
To judge and publicly shame, across Nations

There in a flash, these human behaviors, reactions
viewed in a 30 second tick, or 3 minute reel,
An instant punishment that, to me, at times,
seems worse than death

And so I say to you, Karen
I am sorry – sorry that your perfectly good name
has been tarnished in such a way,
destained to remain derogatory
Knowing that your name, Karen
could have easily been my own, in my younger years
When only talk could describe my bad reaction
to a situation, triggered by the trauma that only
happened moments before, or hours earlier, or years
prior, that moment fading quickly away –
the re-run only in my mind
As others forget, wrapped up in their own stories
their memory of that moment, no longer good gossip

Karen, the stone that is cast unfairly upon you
if I could stop it, I would
I would take the hit to the head, put away the phone
and kindly ask "Karen, are you ok?"
How can I help, how can I help you
get through this moment
If helping means me walking away, I will
If helping means letting you walk away, then I will

I promise you Karen – I promise I will stand composed
with compassion in my heart, I will not poke or prod
I will not take out my phone, press re-cord
No Karen, I will not – I will simply stand in grace until
you or I walk away, so that the talk will gently fade
and the re-run plays only in your mind,
no longer good gossip

And a week from now or a month from then
or even years later
when you find yourself standing in front of yourself,
in younger years,
leave that phone in your pocket,
stand composed, under grace
and pay the kindness forward

CAST OFF

I cast off the thoughts
That do not belong to me
Limiting the talking boxes
They come in many forms
Disguised, in plain sight
I hear now my own voice
Influenced only by introspection
I cast off the sound bites
The half-truths, the far from the truth
The inferences
I cast off the flickering images
The chopped up silent film
Photoshopped with layers of deceit
and bold type letters
None of it is real, none of it reality
I place my bare foot
Onto the mossy green
Then the other
Stretch my arms up to the blue
Turn my gaze upon the swaying trees
The leaves dance and play with the wind
My ears perked to the screeching red-tail
The buzz of bumble and fly
The step of hoof and snapping twig
The water flowing from brook to pond
Firmly I am planted to the earth
Where mystery, magic, and truth
Needs no "thumbs up"

AGING

There is a curve in the hip
Rounded the thigh
Flesh abounds with freckles in toe
Breasts fall, embracing the belly
Twenty will never come around again
Youth fades as age brings many changes
A mirror tells no lies
But lies need no telling
Only judgement needs modification

APOLOGIES

I had so much hope for you little book
Yet.. I set you upon the shelf
There, the dust collected,
Along with all the other, barely filled pages
of many empty books
How I do like holding you in my hands, perfectly sized
Shall we try again?
As I spent some pretty little pennies
on yet another perfect pen

A MILLION PIECES

There are pieces of Me in pieces of You
Not by blood or DNA: that is where
the connection is lost
Following lines that cut us off from all others
From plant, from animal
There are pieces of You in pieces of Me
Feel the tug?
Pulling us towards connection
The web stretches, from fingers to toes
from womb to breast, celestial dust trapped
glistening like dew, in the complexity of microscopic
particles, bits, molecules
We are not separate but rather, separated
by only a thread – still connected
There is a piece of Hawk in a piece of You
You know this – that desire to soar – to fly
You dreamt it… remember?
You continue to dream it
We have hurtled through space,
collided with stars, exploded into a million pieces
scattering through all the ages
There are pieces of You in pieces of all the Suns,
the Moons, the planets
All the flora, the fauna
All the beasts, the birds, the fish
There are pieces of You in pieces of Me
And so, I must love you
And so – I must love myself

SECRETS OF A PAIN FILLED BODY

Pain receptors fire off
Stabbing the rips, a sting, a tingle
A bite here and there
Yet – still I get up
Flat footed burning
Where an arch should be
Gentle joking poking – holy hell that hurts
Yet – still I smile and laugh
This is not old age
My body has ached for 51 years
I have said it aloud – told the doctors
From my womb to my toes
From soft tissue to bone
How it flares, then disappears and flares again
Yet – still I stretch the stiff tired joints
Crack the knees – it is an audible crackling
This is not new – it has always been
I no longer speak of it – not very often…
How it hurts to be touched
And so, I stand guarded and distant
… still longing for touch
I have learned to fight my way through it
I have learned how to move in silence
As most Women do – as most doctors imply…
It's all in the head
I no longer take their tonics, their brews
Their so-called mood altering, mind numbing cures

It is not my mood that causes my pain
It is the pain that effects my mood
(they have it all wrong)

I have grown accustomed to pain
Accepted its presence and simply get up,
move with it throughout my day
No pain, no gain – right?
No pain, hard to imagine
It has always been

ABOUT THE AUTHOR

Not much more can be said about this author that has not already been revealed within these pages. This self-published collection of poetry, small as it is, spans many years. Published really, for the author herself. If one should happen upon it, the hope is, they find meaning and perhaps, inspiration.

Carrie Ann Wall was born and raised in Buffalo, New York and currently resides in a small town in upstate New York.

Email: carriewall22@yahoo.com

Made in the USA
Columbia, SC
03 April 2024